Owning the Moon

Owning the Moon

Linda Sillitoe

Signature Books | 2017 | Salt Lake City

*To all those who traveled the mountains of Utah
and the deserts of Arizona with me.* —L. S.

Cover design by Haden Hamblin

First edition 2017. Copyright Signature Books Publishing
LLC. Signature Books is a registered trademark. All rights
reserved. Printed in the USA on paper certified by the
Sustainable Forestry Initiative. www.signaturebooks.com.

LIBRARY OF CONGRESS CATALOGING-IN-PUBLICATION DATA

Names:	Sillitoe, Linda, 1948–2010, author.
Title:	Owning the moon / Linda Sillitoe.
Description:	First edition. | Salt Lake City : Signature Books, 2017.
Identifiers:	LCCN 2017046519 | ISBN 9781560852667 (alk. paper)
Subjects:	| LCGFT: Poetry.
Classification:	LCC PS3569.I447 O96 2017 | DDC 811/.54—dc23 LC record available at https://lccn.loc.gov/2017046519

Contents

To own, we believe what we see

Love is what it is, not what it says

Do not shuttle corpse dust to infect the moon

Tonight, the moon's as near and far as you

To own, we believe
what we see

Abundance

On the most improbable day – June
in January, a Saturday free –
why are we even talking about
probabilities. As if the russet brush,
shoving its way through old snow
on the splotched hills, is metered.

If we believe in unmetered four-letter
words like time, work, love, (well, money
expands any form, so five letters),
why are we even talking
as the road plunges and twists under
the indifferent tires like an omen.

Here is light lavished on crusted-snow
mountains as if no one counts Saturdays
or money. Sun drenches the scene
that stays frozen, sears the dry road
unrolling beyond sight. Why are we even
announcing our landmarks and deadlines

on a day that unfolds like pages.
Is it so hard to believe in abundance:
that Saturdays abound, that no one
surveyed the canyon and printed the sum.
Or do we place markers rather than see
the sun spilling and ask: *why are we?*

Saturday supper

Young girls and childless women turn and stare
at her weekly march to an empty, in-front pew –

streaky blond and carrot, strawberry, tow,
copper, auburn, dark blond – for it's her share

of glory, at the end, youngest riding
her hip, next swinging heavy within. Bright-

faced children brushed with Sunday light
renew her for another week of sliding

on discarded learning spools, blinking DON'T WALK
down stairs with scissors in your mouth; kisses

that gum her cheek all afternoon, near-misses,
Band-aids, piano, swimming, silly talk.

Pretending shipwreck she rations Saturday's supper
wondering if mother's milk now tracks her veins.

Northerly winds persist in blowing south,
she tells the crew sharing her peanut butter.

Becalmed on a noisy ship among these brains
that startle, breakable wings, eternal mouths.

Song of the pack

While listening through a lecture,
I speculate about men,
their similar cadence and timing,
their liking for running in packs.

Along the front row hunches the pack,
men who track the lecture's timing
and nod, rubbing their beards. The lecture
is on an author, so we hear that man's

prose in phrases that echo the timing
of my longtime friend, a writer, and the man
who taught the speaker behind the lectern.
I see a thread ravel to lasso the pack.

Some of my best friends are men,
but only now do I see how their timing
suckles them, lecture by lecture,
until each lifts the night song of the pack.

Metaphysics over lunch

English professor and rebel:
Off campus, our sentences race
the tabletop, garbed in wit and color.
By the time food comes, our ideas dance
in lines, weaving outrageous figures,
slapping hand on hand. *Nothing can get you
if you don't believe in it*, you say
from safety. And I believe you.

Tribal leader and painter:
An apple in the truck, and we stand
at noon before your glassed-in relative,
dead and reconstructed, her history
on a card. Dug-up death pours off her
and I move away; you stand and read.
Filter, you tell me back at the truck;
stare down what you see without eyes.

Lawyer and fairytale expert:
Now you, astride in your own light,
enjoy lunching in the mountains
where it all sings – snow, mist, or sun.
Your talk treks the high trails;
I inspect shadows where, you say,
nothing we see first can assault us.
Look out, I say as protection.

epilogue
Except when the tab is paid, we don't
consider your long legs bent under
table or steering wheel. We never recall
those priestly hands passing on powers
you may ignore. Is it only my hidden stance
(in Bible and Constitution) that senses
the hollows where everything waits and yearns.

Owning the Moon

Having moved

You settle in as if you designed
the towering eucalyptus trees
that dust a cobalt sky. You learn
the names of neighbors – jacaranda,
ocotillo, devil's claw – and study
the desert doves that hop unnamed.

Having loved too hard, too many,
you sleep alone with one hand on the wall;
your inner space becomes inviolate.
Yet even here the night trains rush
through town blaring the old song:
Coming through! Coming now!

Coming in!

Fact of my life

My job was once threatened if I published a poem.
I lived in another place
but in America and knew my rights.
I let the poem wait. Oh, I read it aloud once
and silence swelled in the room like fog;
then someone said, *Read it again.*

My job was once threatened if I published a poem,
a fact of my life I forgot,
one my children don't know.
A journalist, sworn to truth, nothing but,
I wrote it at City Desk
unassigned to the story.

My job was once threatened if I published a poem
for a public figure, no libel there,
nothing false or obscene, only love
and anger, dignity and crumbs.
The second time I read it, silence rose
and his relative, who questioned me later.

After I left my job I published the poem,
then left the place and forgot
the threat. Remembering, I ponder
the knots lodged under my shoulder blades,
wondering whether one truly can leave a place
where poems hold such power.

First summer in Phoenix

How in triple-digit heat
do common day lilies
stand straight on their roots
and sing? – or lantana blooms
crowd the baking sidewalk,
bobbing with tiny butterflies?

Every sentence you speak
drags a tail tonight.
Some tails have grown back
so often I find no energy
to snap them off again. I only pair
the darker thoughts

with mauve offerings, peach,
and maize. The pairs march now
like allies into your phone;
clearly this is insufficient.
Bad luck, you say, to have opened
your heart in this half-year
to a rounder, an enforcer,
a child molester, and now
a motorcyclist who rejects you
for not loving guns enough.
Bad luck to have named each
only after he stole your wind.

Let me step outside where
apricot clouds shimmer along
a still-blue sky, and moon
lights a shy smile overhead

though fire still flows up from asphalt
all night, the pool warm as a bath.

Among lovely improbables, I dream
danger: *I fortify the house*
only to find an odd menace within
that singes yellow patches on skin;
a rosy infant cooks like a yolk
in my arms and dies. Uncover

uncover the cause! – but others see only
the marks on my face, my urgency
to do something, do something, do –
I wake to another day's scorch, and yet
this afternoon on a seamless blue sky
a chord of rainbow shines. And flowers sing.

Slant sonnet for Melissa

This visit, you talk of Merlin in poem and prose,
and how he transformed Arthur to insect or mole,
teaching him how to become.
                                        And you, briar rose,
bright-petalled and wild, don't I watch you unfold
again and again, dropping bits of yourself without heed,
then offering a thief only a handful of thorns.

In seasons of water, you enter the dolphin who sleeks
past in moonlight; then a falcon who waltzes the sun.
And always your song of the moment spirals and peaks
as if it is truly your last; as if you are one
and not minion; or as if you will deign to repeat
a monotonous chorus.

                                        Who, next visit, will come
as my daughter, carnate, incarnate, only the same
in the glimpse of Merlin flickering behind the flame.

Interruptions

I almost interrupted
when a white magpie
with black accents
returned and leaned
on the restaurant window
for minutes near my hands.

I had been told that when
a bird, insect, or animal
breaks its pattern, you know
the day has cracked like china,
the ocean sprung a leak,
someone died to you. Beware.

More white than black, hawk size,
the bird drew my eyes hard and long
enough – almost – to halt the flow
of postponed words, a hasty plan.
I didn't know, even finding white cars
and dark police for an unattended death.

He left on an undrawn breath
while his cat erupted and the magpie
flew off like nothing. I only knew
it was time to meet my son, who vanished
to a vigil by the body. Here, we offered
shattered words beside that stillness.

We meant love and goodbye, already flown.

Downtown powwow after rain

The vendors' tents go up first –
the commuting Zuni, Apache, Pima,
Acoma Pueblo, Hopi, and Navajo –
then pots, jewelry, t-shirts, key chains,
and dream-catchers to draw the shoppers.
Someone's cassette of powwow songs
rebukes the storm too late for dancing.
Rain has pounded the arena into red clay,
a mire for moccasins and Reeboks.
People begin to leave – maybe tomorrow.
A small girl in a crimson jingle dress
trudges away trailing a fading tinkle.

Before long, drumbeats boom from a parking plaza,
a song rises and holds in the damp air.
Between two rows of parked vehicles
the drumming singers open their throats,
and the gourd dancers form dipping lines.
Watchers press between the vehicles:
various Cherokees and Navajos with feathers
dangling from their rearview mirrors.
One wizened dancer, shuffling with a rattle
and eagle feather fan, may have known
this dance's birth among the code talkers
and discharged soldiers, unemployed

again in the dusty Southwest, shaking
pebbles in a tin can and resurrecting glory.

Again honor soars for warriors in their own
and their conqueror's battles, until the drum
causes the concrete shelves around it
to sound the brave beat. The ugly structure pulses,
a great heart pumping sound into the city.
Then whistles trill, and spirit flies
into everything from this dim passage.

Even cement grows from intent and something
live. Even now the beating heart won't die.

Pay as you go

When you become no more than a car in traffic,
your mind steals out of line and the semaphores
shimmer with tears. No one sees. In ten minutes
you will arrive and park, your words ready;
but in this moment *someone throws open a door*
and you turn – ah! everyone's home at last.
The light turns, your foot presses down. A radio
man advises financial planning to control the future.

Perhaps you should grieve in advance, so no coming loss
can take you unaware. But, as with money, the past
and present quarrel for more than you can dispense.

Someday you'll have time for another destination:
a wailing wall where sound ruptures the clouds;
a canyon bonfire consuming the dross with flames
that leap high as desert varnish on a stone wound.
Someday you'll dance or run this to earth, lie panting
and empty, waiting for rain, or strength, or rescue.
For now, pay the installments, years of road time
in anonymous lanes to see your mourning done.

Long distance

So now you sit with a black eye
by a glass wall on the sixteenth floor.
Already I see our talk in paragraphs
I can't read, topics in the margins,
one clear sentence about clutter.

You didn't warrant the bruised eye
that gazes out the glass wall.
Through it loom the fortresses
of the world's only true church
remarkably outside your north window.

The west window reaches the silver lake,
the mountains, and planes plotting
their patterns like a squadron of gulls.
My hand rose to encircle as you cross-
examined a poem, a lawyer with the answers.

Later, alone, I find it again in my hand:
here, the black eye and the head-on shot
no one can dodge; over there, horizon,
open as a hand curled around a moment;
only a breath beyond glass, the sky.

About grim brothers

If you find in their pages the beauty
whose drink is doctored by a beast;
the princess who wakes to liberate
a kingdom; the girl shoving a witch
into the oven to rescue her brother,

then I see the knight beheading
a dragon to kiss the princess awake;
the dwarf stomping a hole; the prince
vetting a glass shoe. The women only
extend a foot. Or sleep. Or cry. Or guess.

True, wicked stepmothers tarnish their crystals,
poison red apples, and abandon kids in the woods.
But where are those waifs' kindly fathers?
Who makes the sister of swans responsible
to knit nettle sweaters for her brothers?

With one wing un-sleeved, guess who complains?

Afternoon sun

Hope hurts like a blast of sunlight.
Lately you had forgotten that,
striving to think you can cope
with your child's diminished life
even as you dish out potions.

Then one day when she can't
hold up her head as you drive
ten miles to the doctor's office,
he tries something else –
and she reads you a medical piece

on the way home. She sits up.
You both resist joy, stopping
to buy chocolate, carelessly adding
blood-red carnations. They transfuse
her hands as you drive, for colors

she says, burn through the gridlock.
You know she's mentally stacking
the month's backlog she will clear
before it's too late again. But maybe
this will last; no, don't think it.

You can't hope yet, though sunlight
floods your walk like blessings.
Anyone can see the sun hovers
near the horizon and will sink. But now
it pours as hot and true as noon.

Sun to the south

November, and the sun's arc
is small and southerly,
impossibly so; only a stealthy
white rainbow traces day after day.
Rays duck under the balcony,
peer through the windows for hours.

Oh, the world doesn't mind
this balmy November
when electric stars rise
in the trees and huge roses open.
Bell ringers at every outlet
clang it: *Sun to the south*!

Don't offer me science, a tangle
of angles and reasons, until
her white hands full of pills
let her feet dance as they did.
Bring me a rose wide as my palm,
vermillion, and speaking it true:
Open – the air is a gift now,
light at a slant, sun to the south.

Snapshots

Half the scenes I draw on now
happened in odd, haloed moments
irrespective of year or subject:

Ella singing scat in a college gym;
a bereaved ice skater spinning
like a phoenix, hurling defiant sparks
my weakened daughter swallows.

My boy pitching endless strikes
to thank the sky after an auto crash;
a daughter, small and blond with a bullhorn,
shouts down neo-Nazis on public ground.

A hand leaves the gear shift to enclose mine
while outrunning a mountain blizzard;
and you, sunlit at a canyon restaurant,
open book after book I'm going to need.

Love is what it is,
not what it says

White space

For moments after we talk,
a silence thickens
between mouth and mouthpiece
tying both ends of the line
until we manage goodbye.

How does it halt and hold us?
We could try to say more
or feel less. No, leave it
to savor later –

that eloquence.

Advice on love

Never fall for
a wizard, my child,
(and you are just the type,
wise and young,
wanting always to know).

Oh, he'll open the blossoms
to tunnels that sear
your spine and empty
into sky; he'll teach you
to decipher clouds
and nervous laughter,
the snarls in your soul.

But as your eyes remain yours —
not merely his reflection —
with an angry pouf
(or without) he'll disappear
leaving you with the vapors
that drip the insipid message
that it's maybe for your good
(not to mention his convenience).

You'll be walking with sensate feet
in the scatterbrained world,
knowing how to dial him up
when there's no answer, mad to try,
and spoiled just a bit
for ordinary men.

Mutiny

My hand brushed yours –
you took it –
and then we couldn't let go.

Those palms and fingers spoke
all we wouldn't say
for months, maybe years.

Faster than a keyboard,
they seared paragraphs,
pages, symphonies,
flashing through melded flesh
while, wordless, we crossed town.

How did we ever let go,
carry each hand off to cool
in a day tipped out of kilter
and resonant with truth.

Killdeer everywhere

Blue the sky,
as if rain never spilled
the creek below us,
brown and rampant down the spillway,
boiling over rocks.

Green the trees,
as if spring always comes,
rising like a broad
impulsive hymn.

Light lavished here,
to leave the whole world dim;
light spikes the creek,
traces filaments,
a long breath from their pods.

Then winding down the canyon,
a million new-sprung leaves
infused with green,
and lit

too green to burn
but lit,
held hard
and green
and burning.

Saguaro lake

The day after we visited Saguaro Lake,
someone drowned;
then his limbs danced a loose ballet
out of reach.
Not far from him, the land of cactus
rose in flame
near Red Mountain, brittlebush and poppies
torched as tinder.

Our afternoon, the traffic was in birds:
hummingbirds, ducks,
a blur of scarlet as we talked. Seven eagles
hunted the deep red cliffs,
tracing circles above the cholla, whose needles
cupped the light.
Nearer earth, birds winged around the secrets
we cached in the air.

Computer art

Here is the scene: a dry desert mountain
with a rock outcrop a ways from the road,
a distant city below, partly cloudy sky,
no wildlife but someone's door-in
and door-out like hollow eyes in the dirt,
and, on the boulder, a woman and man.

They have perspective on the smoggy city,
the planes nosing between skyscrapers,
but turn tensely toward each other, talking.
Try this: leave him where he is and move her
to that ledge across a gulch. They still look
toward each other – as wish or estrangement,

beginning or end? Now manipulate the scene
degree by degree until their angles change
and they singly gaze at the city below,
in solitude or loneliness. Yes.   No, turn them
back. Cancel, cancel. Return to the original.
Only their proximity highlights the details:

the unlocked vehicle angled off the road
where a javelina pokes a contraband carton.
Only now does sun gleam from that stone,
a silence enfold them, the mountain plunge
steeply. See the pebbles that skid underfoot
and, as they rise, the grip of their hands.

Owning the Moon

Violin

We begin on the D string,
warm and mellow,
amber brooks gamboling
under mild sunlight;
hands on skin,
skin on skin;
      move to the A's
sincerity, a rise in pitch,
of tongues and lips,
reaching for the high notes.

Then rough strokes on G,
the fierceness that thrills
without peril, the chase
through dark that only runs
faster, faster, up stairs
and down, around triumphant corners;

then on E, silver sweet,
a poignance stealing
breath and thought,
impossible note by note
by note
until that light touch
and the octave sings –
erupting sunrise,
flame across the sky.

Withdrawal

Absent, you are everywhere at once:
in the chair (angled as you left it),
putting on your shoes,
lifting a cup of tea;

and where the wall turns, you begin a smile;
your words replay
upon the shifting air;
eyes closed, you trek

the regions in your head. These holograms, and more,
keep friendly company
to counteract the wish
for you specifically.

Timing

Now you must reclaim all you best forgot:
the way to start the baby crying
when you're lonesome in the dark;
the bowls of water you set out nightly
for little folk who never showed themselves.

Now independent, emerging most yourself,
you become the kitten whose poster you tacked up
all over town. The cats you tried to save
now flare their eyes to guide you through the dark.

Summoned, nixies offer water for your thirst.
The half-dead apple tree you mourned
as kindling spreads a canopy. And irrepressibly
the rocking chair still creaks its song
of someone watching so that you can sleep.

Dream analysis

While absent, you've come in three dreams.
In one, you brought thanks from a prophet
then lectured on securities I didn't understand.
I left thinking we'd meet up later. We almost did.

In another, our lunch came, but yours
was a plate of boiled vegetables and eggs.
One look, and you became restless
but wouldn't send it back or re-order.

In the third, we stood in a lobby discussing
agendas – whether to stay and work
or drive back, talking on the road. I knew
what would transpire either way.

In one of those dreams you held
and kissed me. In one, you avoided
explaining your figures. We decided
only to travel and talk on the way.

Ballad from the wilds

In the wilds of love you seek the other
who's seeking you. In forest, needles fall
to ease the random slope where you take cover.

By sea, the moon bedazzles sight, as salt
sparks everything to flame upon your tongue.

In jungle, you are wary of the beasts,
yet your own pelt rises to your lover's hand.

The desert speaks of all the parching wastes
between; it singes every stone with sunset
and fires the sky as if passion never calms.

You know or guess all this; yet don't expect
to confront behind so many shrubs or palms

unmasked and varied selves: who you were;
who you are; and who you always were.

Do not shuttle corpse
dust to infect the moon

The man who works with nightmares

The nightmares make appointments and come in
clad in human skin and modern clothes,
children hatched by hospitals in casts, steel plates,
and stitches; veterans shocked awake by fusillades;
every kind of rape at any age, now assuming flesh.

He sits the nightmares down; they draw or talk.
His slides will slice the brain to light and show
how trauma splits or lodges but mean less than how
one holds his gaze, the eyes his father brought
from Hitler's camps. If talking chokes, he breathes

his mother's silence. *Terrible things happened
to you*, he says. At once he smells a flare in his office;
cars boom and break; freeways fall; and terrorists' eyes
gleam like automatic weapons. The thrust a child escaped
by disappearing skewers the woman beside him. One by one,

the nightmares teach the scientist how they hurt.
He teaches how to heal, enraging certain nightmares
who read human skin and desire to thrive. They memorize
his voice and prints, then track him everywhere. He skis
powder when he can, seeks red-rock, then goes back to work.

Lost moons

Someone crouches on the steps of a trailer
in Wyoming, watching the sky's chilly wind.
What comfort might that person find, shifting
on metal, to recognize the Wait–until–I–Come–Moon
of the Kiowa in October when the long hunt ends.

More comfort and meaning in Wyoming than Octavius
or Augustus, Julius Caesar or Janus. School out,
who are the Romans to us – living the rhythms
of the New World, compelled by its seas and spaces.
How foolish to have kept the Uncompahgre River,

the Uintah Mountains, Seattle, and Detroit,
(the landscapes scourged of peoples),
yet to have forgotten their moons. Wouldn't our factories
flourish below the Caribou–Abundant–in–the–Woods?
Meteorologists could stop guessing about weather and know

travelers' fates under the Moon–of–Snow–Blindness
or the Moon–When–the–Cold–Makes–Trees–Crack.
Geography would connect like the land if children
imagined the Ojibway filing under the Snow–Crust–Moon
even as the Melting–Snow–Moon gathered Navajos to the dance.

We would wake in the haze of the Plant–in–Secret–Moon,
anticipate languid lovemaking under the Corn–in–Tassel.
Sorrow, borne by the Moon–When–Reindeer–Return–from–the–Sea,
or hunger below the Cold–Meal–Moon, would fit like lost skin
if each year thundered forth the Moon–When–the–Buffalo–Ruts.

Wrong conversation

First you spoke your diagnosis
over the pink tablecloth
at a Vietnamese restaurant –
radical surgery or early death.
Both of us shocked, right then
we pursued the wrong conversation.

I resolved in every encounter after
to offer a change of subject. Wryly,
you reported the doctors calling you
compliant, improving your chances.
Truly you chose their difficult melody,
I knew, from the alto in your voice.

But would you have just told me
you were leaving if the doctors,
if dear ones, didn't score the song?
And my own alto crooned, *Don't go, don't go,*
even as I longed to see, not the travel ads
but your journey through the jungle.

Hospital healing

Of course a two-inch badger
carved from liver-colored stone
with arrows bound to his back
could not make the difference.

The day I brought him, you couldn't
talk. The next, weaker, yellow,
you gasped your question. Death held
your other hand while I bluffed.

The badger, I said, *travels the dark*
world below, then surfaces again.
(Later I learned he oversees healing.)
You watched him, you tell me now,

like a reddish star in a poisoned sky.
Home now, in a pink sweater,
you claim, thereby dazzling me,
not the badger but your own life.

Imposter

Outside of church
you say you hate the god
ranting this scripture and that
like the leader of a cult.

As you speak, God glitters
along the leaves,
hovers by a nest,
and rests in your dark eyes
that still unsee the followers
who howled your fierce
conception on the night
when devils rage.

You – handed past
the girl raped on the altar –
still harbor that same light
of God silking the leaves
and tending nests,
seeing everything
the faithful will unsee.

Arizona wind

The wind's howl
must rise from far off,
rushing the Salt River's dry bed,
screaming its protest.

Is this a choir of ghosts
blown south from the caves
near Hopi mesas where bones
of their ancestors sing?

What, near my urban pueblo,
justifies the crescendo and roar
of the dry gusts now shaking
the jacaranda trees like rags,

mummifying the afternoon shoppers
in strip malls as they straggle
to their cars. No day for pools:
two-year-old twins drowned yesterday.

Has the wind come for them? –
small exhibits in the ongoing debate
over fence types and laws.
What does the wind want,

wailing anew, dragging its sleeves
and hem along adobe and concrete,
plucking the last jacaranda blooms
like twins fathoming latches at last.

Mourning a redhead, a collector of pigs

Mourning you finds so little focus, stretching empty
        as a winter meadow or a row of white
        calendar days with nothing circled,
an ache as plain and crucial as the air we drew at lunch,
week by week, a two-way oral history, now gone out of print.

I remind myself that when I clutched the phone,
        as a mutual friend described your sudden death,
        a redheaded bird perched opposite
my window, staring in at me for minutes; then it sprang
into flight so gleeful, I had to laugh. The way we laughed.

This holiday I shop for a pig to hang beside my tree:
        it flaunts a dress and wings, it holds a bell.
        One winter you cussed every time I kicked
the bell on your car's floor. Nightly you braved snowdrifts to ring
that bell so certain girls inside would not quit Santa Claus.
        For you, I ring it now.

August in Phoenix

Cicada-loaded trees buzz like snakes.
    Rain marries the air
        until neither is itself.
All that falls is a doctor's dice,
    a pattern we knew
        that he now marks in blood.
August, an escalator whose stairs
    flatten as I climb
        yet rise like morning.
For months, summer has sulked,
        and you more silent than God.

Broken sonnet

Something vital vanished from the landscape
when you died after work and before supper.
Not old, not sick, but gone. Now your laughter
echoes as from another room; you recap
arguments of practicalities.

*A secret is something you tell one person at
a time*, you'd tease, *and it's not what you like that
makes you fat*. But do clues lurk in these?
They say you left to fill an urgent call
as if urgency exists outside of time.

I, your pagan daughter, said nothing formal,
only slid one clear, small stone inside
your burial robes. It's for your journey taken,
Dad, your journey still.

Carlos Nakai at Litchfield Park

One man and a flute begin.
Trees lean through their light to listen.
Under the bandstand, below the folding chairs,
the land awakes, rippling toward the blue Estrellas.
The land recalls how notes unwind and yearn,
courting the sun. One man in quills
and buckskin. One flute in the morning.

Now a slant of eagle bone slides
between his lips, and this bone shrills
an eagle's heart, an eagle's eye,
thin air, a wind that curls and spirals,
the lift of flight like sinew in the wings.
The sky leans in as this white bone
sings every cell it knows,
                    and cries
                    and cries
                    and cries.

Tonight, the moon's as
near and far as you

(

Is there a moon?

If you call me at nine some night,
you say, and I ask after the moon,
you can answer without looking.
You explain over lunch how one body
revolves around another, and when.

Stubborn and silent, my mind snags: *if
you call, would I ask?* For the moon lives
so near me in another state, it's my
middle name. Driving home today, the moon
looks from the east at quarter before five,

an opaque face on warm blue sky.
See – I note the time, its height,
and think of you. If you call, I'll ask.

A genie's complaint

You called me up: story on the screen,
voices across wires; of course I felt
your hands rubbing the lamp.
                    I took your gifts,
the high-held torch, the accurate flung stone,
and tendered what you wished: clearly to see
your face alight, your stance within the play.

You respond and shouldn't, you now say?
But this is what I do when conjured free.
This is real, the heartland of a dream.
For this, you search the files, tap in numbers,
flare a little magic, call it modern-day,
and all the time you know intent's the game.
Better to leave your electric hands in slumber
than to summon me and smile, then turn away.

Legacy

I'm enough your daughter to acknowledge
my easy lot. I have friends whose fathers died
before she could be crowned rodeo queen,
or he be elected to student office, or she
leave her own hospital bed. One friend's dad
died, while traveling, from a diabetic coma;
doctors ignored "another drunk Indian"; not like
you were pummeled, or like friends' fathers
chilling slowly, forcing their children's hard bloom.

Lucky, I grew up to know you couldn't fix everything
except with laughter, hearty with glee or chagrin.
I claim luck now in this forsaken world:
so many items broke when you died.

For now

For now, neither the morning nor I
am captive. We move carelessly.
The cat snoozes in the curl of the quilt,
knowing I can't make my bed.
My daughter sleeps so soundly
she may wake whole again.
The neighbors have left,
the small boy's voice piping
behind him like ebbing traffic.

And despite a week's forecast
of clouds and rain, for now
the sky invents brilliant blue.
A sun ray flings a diagonal
across my keys, my work.
I must work and work well
on this empty beach of morning
that promises like a lover's goodbye,
hoping soon, meaning *now*.

Sensing spirits

We had to fly to her brother's wedding.
But she lay prone on a heating pad,
the room spinning above, and her
weight and blood pressure stuck below
one hundred. I prepared to carve
her pink bridesmaid's dress to fit,
then sew it smooth and smaller.

I hoped the sounds of a native flute might ease
the unforgiving fabric and erase
my fear of a misshapen dress walking
her down the aisle – if she could walk.
One seam sewn, I took a breath
and went to check the patient.
I'm fine, she chirped, *don't worry*.

Pilgrim is circled here on my chest.
Aunt Fern is helping you fix my dress.
I gasped and said, *That's good.*
Fern died when I was twelve. This daughter ate
my memories more than food, which turned
her inside out. Pilgrim, her feline nursemaid,
had been put to sleep. And our new cat,

young and lionesque, skirted the sickroom.
That day, the tension I tried to hide haloed
me like burrs, too thick for sensing spirits.
But I was glad for her unless it meant …
Oh, let me edit that aching day with vision:
not homecoming, her knees sharp through denim
as a wheelchair bore her through the airport;

not the months and pounds and pressure points
yet to fall like long brown hair before her bones
finally turned on a solid diagnosis. Let me glimpse
her kicking off white shoes – as she did – to dance
with her new nephew, so suave in his small tux.
Let me know I'll pump the camera to invest
her macarena whirl against whatever comes.

Return to the Rockies

We returned to our beginnings
        in August, with its crayon green
        trees and grass, blue sky,
and yellow light so certainly imposed
that desert light and night and hues
        wavered within us.

We settled near the mountains,
        opening our windows
to crickets wooing a canyon breeze.
        We tried to believe
we can fit in this time among our dearest
and darkest demons. We unpacked and sorted
        our souvenirs and tales

of treading the back trails we tread still
even as we merge into traffic.
        People don't request those stories.
They say, *Welcome back*
        to this, the right place.
Crickets translate:
        About time.

Encounter

Absently I opened the medicine cabinet
in my folks' house (searching for a comb),
then stood stunned as you wafted out
like a genie, so generous with cologne
and after-shave I glanced behind me.
The room wavered like my knees.

Staring into that worn square of shelves,
I wondered, *Has she kept everything?*
Two years later, even your shaving brush
bristles from its cup amid the scents
of you spruced up, agenda laid, ready to go.
Alone, does she press this latch to summon you,
who left without giving notice? Will it
ever become easier to let you out the door?

Afterward

Far west from the towers that fell,
the leaves keep changing, bright yellow
into old gold, orange to russet, red to burgundy.

The local fighter jets transform – from too-costly
toys that roar precision tricks around their base –
to drilling athletes, hunters, guardians of the nation.

The other change creeps stealthily indoors
where we tune our fear by color, shake our mail,
and hate the threatening whine of even little planes.

Neighbors near a flight school

Later, we knew who they were,
those neat, quick neighbors
who never nodded or said hello
as we passed between cars.

Always in pairs, faces closed as if
we offended as women, or with laundry.
Despite so many broad windows,
I avoided doing laundry at night.

Never a blue morning worth greeting
if we met them on the stairs. Meanwhile we
gathered with friends downtown for Chinese
New Year or Hopi hoop dancing; seated low

in Patriot Park or beside the Heard Museum,
our eyes rose irresistibly to jets that seemed
to dodge between buildings. Later, we understood
those hostile eyes, the roar of jets, dust waiting to fall.

In April

Spring was always your season. We monitored
lilacs and tulips to behead each of them
for your birthday breakfast. If you wished a few
spared in the garden, you didn't complain.

                      This first raw year
when you miss the delicate infusion of green in new leaves,
the first spring when pollens can't stalk you, I count daffodils
again for you, as your grandchildren picnic on a blanket
on one Saturday too warm to last through April.

                      I read in my siblings' eyes
the shadow cast in January on the day we sped like orphans
to the hospital: each trying to park; each knowing you left
in a heartbeat, like Dad; each fearing they would drag you
halfway back; each hoping for time to speak again our love.

You played so dead that noon, then again, and again.
Above the picnic, a chatter of birds sublets the trees,
and you sparkle, undiminished, and barely
                      beyond the spring.

Spinning empty-handed

I have reinvented prayer for your peril,
shaped my own departed into saints
and winged them to your aid. Do you sense
their phrases swaddling you? Or does my smoke
from sage and sweet grass circle you at night?

Still, you walk your cliff, eyes in your toes.
I say, *You've always had those eyes*. You say,
I know. You think I've never loved a demon
as you love yours, nor kept my feet alert
to the abyss.

               I must be centered like the pole
from which trapeze and tightrope spring to air,
high and free. So I stand empty-handed,
spinning below you nets – and nets, and nets.

Overlooked

You have forgotten that morning –
so had I – under a wild gray sky
when red hills opened like a wound.
We walked until we came to a ravine
and stood watching ravens catch
the thermals, yell, and sail across.

We weren't there first; human debris
crusted the ground, walking back. We left
only whatever we said where everything ached.
Now I find it enough, you and I overlooking
the abyss from the same air pocket,
wordless, watching ravens ride the wind.

Urban madonna

After work she hails the last bus home
and dozes to her stop; she jerks awake
as if an infant's cry rose in the storm.
Protected by her legs, no one could take
the bags she gathers now; umbrella out,
she disembarks to squares of stained-glass ice.
She pays the sitter, then her children's doubts
of Santa torment them like anxious mice.

She snacks until they settle then retrieves
her Singer, puts it by the lamp. Her years
unwind in rhythm, as cloth and needle weave
her daughters' dreams. When midnight nears,
she twists into her hair a twig of holly
like some indentured elf beside the tree.

Fifteen months

For Susan

Twin homemade coats, red against the snow,
yours sewn a little larger – you lorded time
as if age held awards that months denied.

Two violins, shared resin for the bows,
a Sunday pact to share forgiveness–es;
and yet in junior high you swept by wordless
through the halls. A senior, you counted kisses;
I counted boys who kissed; you snatched my roses
and slashed the stems away to fit a vase.

We ran so hard, shared decades always full,
as if running witnessed some salvation's cost
we otherwise couldn't pay. Who calls this race,
as I bring flowers you said all should withhold?
The line means losing first – or being lost.

Oasis

At dusk the pool waits in silence,
found by your feet after you rip up
the map. Suddenly in tangled grasses
and twilight the birds stop calling,
and the trees finger your face.

You shed your jacket, drop the rod
that measures a son lost to highway
or gun, a daughter to cancer or fist,
a parent to diapers and bibs, each
ending the wrong size and time.

In this clearing, your story is known
without words, where the logic twists
from sight. Everything pools and settles.
And then the pond of blood becomes water,
cold and real; we kneel at its edge to drink.

Owning the moon

i.
Its broad face fills my east window.
Tonight you are east, not north,
so the moon looks over you
toward me, yet noses the glass.

Once I dreamed our talks were tied
in separate packages, my name
written on each – but the name
no one knows, my moon name.

I told you this dream years before
you claimed that we each own the moon
in part, years before we wondered
if we own anything at all.

ii.
To own, we believe what we see –
shiny disc, yellow grin, ivory smudge –
not photos of craters and dust.
We sense the sea lift toward

the moon's trail and Earth quiver
as we do on axis. Maybe lunacy
rides on such nights, but love
is what it is, not what it says.

Besides, the cliffs open below
a full moon, no more improbable
than trekking a planet that spins,
where passion is holy as anything.

iii.
Let the moon be our covenant then,
seen or not, shape-shifting by day
and dark, yet constant in its disguise.
Let the moon be a shining fulcrum

between two creatures of disowned
lineage who have found some camouflage.
Perhaps the moon is all love can be:
misunderstood, mis-trekked, mis-claimed,

while below we learn Hollywood's tale,
applied with glue in our hometown. Always,
the moon sang its ballads in silence,
whirling us round and round.

iv.
Do not shuttle, the Navajos say,
this corpse dust to infect the moon.
Notice the banished there now
who infiltrate Earth at full moon.

Don't sirens scream? What havoc
will reign if those who claim that
ashes are only ash implant a body's
death to grow and shade the moon.

Tonight, the moon's as near and far as you.
If the moon be dead, will you outlast
its light that trickles through my hands?
You shine inside my eyelids then are gone.

v.

After a period of dark, you rise
with dreams in your hand, stirring
the tides like a wind. I stay inside.
For a time, dark enfolds me, but then

you investigate my window.
Already my traitorous dreams
have shown what we own or lack,
real as the sea preaching solids,

scribbling warranties in the sand.
Over time, we lose what we own
and learn the motions that bring it back –
like this moon, as caught, as wild, as we.

The phases of Linda's life (captions)

CHILDHOOD AND YOUTH

Age three in 1951 near her parents' home in the Liberty Park neighborhood of Salt Lake City, p. 13.

Kindergarten, Liberty Elementary, 1953, p. 73.

Also in 1953, Linda (left) and older sister, Susan, in smiles and homemade dresses, p. 60.

Perched on the tractor at her Uncle Herman and Aunt Rosemarie's Idaho farm in 1955, p. 36.

Linda's success on the debate team in her junior year of high school (1964-65) prepared her for future rebelliousness, p. 47.

MARRIAGE AND FAMILY

Always observing, especially as a journalist at the *Deseret News*, p. 31.

With her husband, John, at his graduation from the University of Utah when he received his master's degree in history, p. 52.

Life was good in 1977. Linda relaxes at a barbecue in her in-laws' backyard, p. 66.

In 1979 at the home where Linda began her career as a freelance journalist and she and John raised their three children, p. 78.

A B C D E F G H I J K L M
N O P Q R S T U V W X Y Z

A B C D E F G H I J K L M
N O P Q R S T U V W X Y Z

A B C D E F G H I J K L M
N O P Q R S T U V W X Y Z

Section titles in *Owning the Moon* are set in Renovation, a brush script by Bulgarian designer Veneta Rangelova. The geometric letters of the poems' titles were designed by Jos Buivenga in 2008 for a typeface called Museo Slab. The text was typeset in Adobe Jenson, a revival of Nicholas Jenson's thirteenth-century font easily identified by its diamond-shaped period.

More poetry from Signature Books

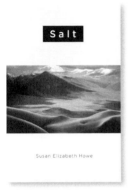

Salt by Susan Elizabeth Howe | $19.95

Her Side of It by Marilyn Bushman-Carlton | $16.95

Some Love by Alex Caldiero | $17.95

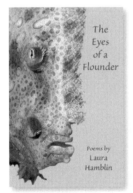

The Eyes of a Flounder by Laura Hamblin | $15.95

Mapping the Bones of the World by Warren Hatch | $15.95